50 Baking to Soothe the Soul Recipes

By: Kelly Johnson

Table of Contents

- Classic Banana Bread
- Chocolate Chip Cookies
- Cinnamon Rolls
- Blueberry Muffins
- Lemon Pound Cake
- Apple Crisp
- Pumpkin Bread
- Fudgy Brownies
- Oatmeal Raisin Cookies
- Strawberry Shortcake
- Coffee Cake with Streusel Topping
- Honey Butter Cornbread
- Buttermilk Biscuits
- Molasses Crinkle Cookies
- Zucchini Bread
- Peach Cobbler
- Snickerdoodle Cookies

- Classic Cheesecake
- Vanilla Cupcakes with Buttercream
- Soft Pretzels
- Chocolate Lava Cakes
- Raspberry Almond Bars
- Orange Poppy Seed Loaf
- Chocolate Chip Scones
- Lemon Bars
- Almond Biscotti
- Sticky Toffee Pudding
- Cherry Clafoutis
- Irish Soda Bread
- Carrot Cake with Cream Cheese Frosting
- Gingerbread Loaf
- Cranberry Orange Muffins
- Apple Pie
- Chocolate Zucchini Cake
- Butterscotch Blondies
- Pineapple Upside-Down Cake

- Coconut Macaroons
- Pumpkin Muffins
- Marble Pound Cake
- Rustic Berry Galette
- Maple Pecan Scones
- Chocolate Babka
- Chai-Spiced Oat Bars
- Bread Pudding
- Lavender Shortbread Cookies
- Cherry Pie Bars
- Almond Cake with Citrus Glaze
- Classic Sugar Cookies
- Sweet Potato Biscuits
- Lemon Ricotta Cookies

Classic Banana Bread

Ingredients:

- 3 ripe bananas (mashed)
- 1/3 cup melted butter
- 1/2 cup sugar
- 1 egg (beaten)
- 1 tsp vanilla extract
- 1 tsp baking soda
- Pinch of salt
- 1 1/2 cups all-purpose flour

Instructions:

1. Preheat oven to 350°F (175°C). Grease a loaf pan.
2. Mix bananas with melted butter. Stir in sugar, egg, and vanilla.
3. Add baking soda and salt, then flour. Mix until just combined.
4. Pour into loaf pan and bake for 50–60 minutes.
5. Cool before slicing.

Chocolate Chip Cookies

Ingredients:

- 1 cup butter (softened)
- 1 cup brown sugar
- 1/2 cup white sugar
- 2 eggs
- 2 tsp vanilla extract
- 2 1/4 cups all-purpose flour
- 1 tsp baking soda
- 1/2 tsp salt
- 2 cups chocolate chips

Instructions:

1. Preheat oven to 375°F (190°C).
2. Cream butter and sugars. Beat in eggs and vanilla.
3. Add dry ingredients and mix. Stir in chocolate chips.
4. Drop by spoonfuls onto baking sheet.
5. Bake 9–11 minutes until golden brown.

Cinnamon Rolls

Ingredients (Dough):

- 1 cup warm milk
- 2 1/4 tsp yeast
- 1/2 cup sugar
- 1/3 cup melted butter
- 2 eggs
- 4 cups flour
- 1 tsp salt

Filling:

- 1/2 cup butter (softened)
- 1 cup brown sugar
- 2 tbsp cinnamon

Icing:

- 4 oz cream cheese
- 1/4 cup butter (softened)
- 1 cup powdered sugar
- 1/2 tsp vanilla

Instructions:

1. Combine milk and yeast. Let sit 5 min. Mix with sugar, butter, eggs, flour, and salt. Knead until smooth.

2. Let rise 1 hour. Roll out and spread with filling. Roll up, cut into 12 pieces.

3. Place in a greased pan and let rise 30 minutes.

4. Bake at 350°F (175°C) for 20–25 minutes. Top with icing.

Blueberry Muffins

Ingredients:

- 1 1/2 cups flour
- 3/4 cup sugar
- 1/2 tsp salt
- 2 tsp baking powder
- 1/3 cup oil
- 1 egg
- 1/3 cup milk
- 1 cup blueberries (fresh or frozen)

Instructions:

1. Preheat oven to 400°F (200°C). Grease a muffin tin or use liners.
2. Mix dry ingredients. In another bowl, whisk oil, egg, and milk.
3. Combine and fold in blueberries.
4. Fill muffin cups 3/4 full. Bake 18–20 minutes.

Lemon Pound Cake

Ingredients:

- 1 cup butter (softened)
- 2 cups sugar
- 4 eggs
- 1/3 cup lemon juice
- 2 tbsp lemon zest
- 3 cups all-purpose flour
- 1/2 tsp baking soda
- 1/2 tsp salt
- 1 cup sour cream

Instructions:

1. Preheat oven to 350°F (175°C). Grease a loaf or bundt pan.
2. Cream butter and sugar. Beat in eggs one at a time.
3. Add lemon juice and zest. Mix in dry ingredients alternately with sour cream.
4. Pour into pan and bake 60–70 minutes. Cool and glaze if desired.

Apple Crisp

Ingredients (Filling):

- 6 apples (peeled and sliced)
- 1/4 cup sugar
- 1/2 tsp cinnamon
- 1 tsp lemon juice

Topping:

- 3/4 cup flour
- 1/2 cup oats
- 1/2 cup brown sugar
- 1/2 cup butter (cold, cubed)
- Pinch of salt

Instructions:

1. Preheat oven to 350°F (175°C).
2. Toss apples with sugar, cinnamon, and lemon juice. Place in baking dish.
3. Mix topping ingredients until crumbly. Sprinkle over apples.
4. Bake 40–45 minutes until bubbly and golden.

Pumpkin Bread

Ingredients:

- 1 3/4 cups flour
- 1 tsp baking soda
- 1/2 tsp salt
- 1/2 tsp cinnamon
- 1/4 tsp nutmeg
- 1/4 tsp cloves
- 1 cup pumpkin puree
- 1/2 cup oil
- 2 eggs
- 1 cup sugar
- 1 tsp vanilla extract

Instructions:

1. Preheat oven to 350°F (175°C). Grease a loaf pan.
2. Mix dry ingredients in one bowl.
3. In another bowl, mix pumpkin, oil, eggs, sugar, and vanilla.
4. Combine wet and dry. Pour into pan and bake 55–60 minutes.

Fudgy Brownies

Ingredients:

- 1/2 cup butter (melted)
- 1 cup sugar
- 2 eggs
- 1 tsp vanilla
- 1/3 cup cocoa powder
- 1/2 cup flour
- 1/4 tsp salt
- 1/4 tsp baking powder

Instructions:

1. Preheat oven to 350°F (175°C). Grease a square baking pan.
2. Mix melted butter and sugar. Beat in eggs and vanilla.
3. Add cocoa, flour, salt, and baking powder.
4. Spread into pan and bake 20–25 minutes. Cool before cutting.

Oatmeal Raisin Cookies

Ingredients:

- 1 cup butter (softened)
- 1 cup brown sugar
- 1/2 cup white sugar
- 2 eggs
- 1 tsp vanilla extract
- 1 1/2 cups flour
- 1 tsp baking soda
- 1 tsp cinnamon
- 1/2 tsp salt
- 3 cups rolled oats
- 1 cup raisins

Instructions:

1. Preheat oven to 350°F (175°C).
2. Cream butter and sugars. Beat in eggs and vanilla.
3. Mix in dry ingredients, then oats and raisins.
4. Drop spoonfuls onto baking sheets and bake 10–12 minutes.

Strawberry Shortcake

Ingredients (Biscuits):

- 2 cups flour
- 1/4 cup sugar
- 1 tbsp baking powder
- 1/2 tsp salt
- 1/2 cup cold butter (cubed)
- 2/3 cup milk
- 1 tsp vanilla extract

Strawberries & Cream:

- 1 lb strawberries (sliced, mixed with 2 tbsp sugar)
- 1 cup heavy cream (whipped with 1 tbsp sugar & 1/2 tsp vanilla)

Instructions:

1. Preheat oven to 425°F (220°C).
2. Mix dry ingredients, cut in butter until crumbly. Stir in milk and vanilla.
3. Drop or cut into 8 biscuits and bake 12–15 minutes.
4. Split, fill with strawberries and whipped cream.

Coffee Cake with Streusel Topping

Ingredients (Cake):

- 1/2 cup butter (softened)
- 1 cup sugar
- 2 eggs
- 1 tsp vanilla
- 2 cups flour
- 1 tsp baking powder
- 1/2 tsp baking soda
- 1/2 tsp salt
- 1 cup sour cream

Streusel:

- 1/2 cup brown sugar
- 1/2 cup flour
- 1 tsp cinnamon
- 1/4 cup butter (cold)

Instructions:

1. Preheat oven to 350°F (175°C). Grease a 9x9 pan.
2. Cream butter and sugar. Add eggs and vanilla. Mix dry ingredients separately.

3. Alternate adding dry mix and sour cream.

4. Pour half in pan, sprinkle with half streusel. Add rest and top.

5. Bake 35–40 minutes.

Honey Butter Cornbread

Ingredients:

- 1 cup cornmeal
- 1 cup flour
- 1 tbsp baking powder
- 1/2 tsp salt
- 1/2 cup butter (melted)
- 1/3 cup honey
- 2 eggs
- 1 cup milk

Instructions:

1. Preheat oven to 375°F (190°C).
2. Whisk dry ingredients in one bowl.
3. Mix butter, honey, eggs, and milk in another.
4. Combine and pour into greased 8x8 pan.
5. Bake 25–30 minutes until golden.

Buttermilk Biscuits

Ingredients:

- 2 cups flour
- 1 tbsp baking powder
- 1/2 tsp baking soda
- 1/2 tsp salt
- 1/2 cup cold butter (cubed)
- 3/4 cup cold buttermilk

Instructions:

1. Preheat oven to 450°F (230°C).
2. Mix dry ingredients. Cut in butter until crumbly.
3. Stir in buttermilk just until combined.
4. Turn onto floured surface, pat into 1-inch thick dough, cut with biscuit cutter.
5. Bake 12–15 minutes.

Molasses Crinkle Cookies

Ingredients:

- 3/4 cup butter (softened)
- 1 cup sugar
- 1 egg
- 1/4 cup molasses
- 2 cups flour
- 2 tsp baking soda
- 1 tsp cinnamon
- 1/2 tsp cloves
- 1/2 tsp ginger
- 1/2 tsp salt
- Extra sugar for rolling

Instructions:

1. Preheat oven to 375°F (190°C).
2. Cream butter and sugar. Beat in egg and molasses.
3. Mix dry ingredients, then combine. Chill dough 30 mins.
4. Roll into balls and coat in sugar.
5. Bake 8–10 minutes until crinkled.

Zucchini Bread

Ingredients:

- 2 cups grated zucchini
- 1 1/2 cups flour
- 1/2 tsp salt
- 1/2 tsp baking soda
- 1/2 tsp baking powder
- 1 tsp cinnamon
- 1/4 tsp nutmeg
- 1 cup sugar
- 1/2 cup vegetable oil
- 2 eggs
- 1 tsp vanilla

Instructions:

1. Preheat oven to 350°F (175°C). Grease a loaf pan.
2. Mix dry ingredients. In another bowl, beat eggs, sugar, oil, and vanilla.
3. Stir in zucchini. Add dry ingredients.
4. Pour into pan and bake 50–60 minutes.

Peach Cobbler

Ingredients (Filling):

- 4 cups sliced peaches (fresh or canned)
- 1/2 cup sugar
- 1 tsp lemon juice
- 1 tsp cinnamon

Batter:

- 1/2 cup butter (melted)
- 1 cup flour
- 1 cup sugar
- 2 tsp baking powder
- 1/4 tsp salt
- 3/4 cup milk

Instructions:

1. Preheat oven to 350°F (175°C). Pour melted butter into baking dish.
2. Mix batter ingredients and pour over butter (don't stir).
3. Toss peaches with sugar and cinnamon, spoon on top.
4. Bake 40–45 minutes until golden.

Snickerdoodle Cookies

Ingredients:

- 1 cup butter (softened)
- 1 1/2 cups sugar
- 2 eggs
- 2 3/4 cups flour
- 2 tsp cream of tartar
- 1 tsp baking soda
- 1/4 tsp salt

Cinnamon Sugar Coating:

- 2 tbsp sugar
- 2 tsp cinnamon

Instructions:

1. Preheat oven to 375°F (190°C).
2. Cream butter and sugar. Add eggs.
3. Mix in dry ingredients.
4. Roll dough into balls, coat in cinnamon sugar.
5. Bake 8–10 minutes until set and crackled.

Classic Cheesecake

Crust:

- 1 1/2 cups graham cracker crumbs
- 1/4 cup sugar
- 1/3 cup melted butter

Filling:

- 4 (8 oz) packages cream cheese (softened)
- 1 cup sugar
- 1 tsp vanilla extract
- 4 large eggs
- 2/3 cup sour cream
- 2/3 cup heavy cream

Instructions:

1. Preheat oven to 325°F (165°C).
2. Mix crust ingredients and press into springform pan. Bake for 10 minutes.
3. Beat cream cheese and sugar. Add vanilla and eggs one at a time.
4. Blend in sour cream and heavy cream. Pour into crust.
5. Bake 55–65 minutes until center is slightly jiggly. Cool and chill for 4 hours or overnight.

Vanilla Cupcakes with Buttercream

Cupcakes:

- 1 1/2 cups flour
- 1 1/2 tsp baking powder
- 1/4 tsp salt
- 1/2 cup butter (softened)
- 1 cup sugar
- 2 eggs
- 2 tsp vanilla
- 1/2 cup milk

Buttercream:

- 1 cup butter (softened)
- 3–4 cups powdered sugar
- 2 tsp vanilla
- 2–4 tbsp milk

Instructions:

1. Preheat oven to 350°F (175°C). Line a muffin tin.
2. Cream butter and sugar. Add eggs and vanilla.
3. Mix in dry ingredients alternating with milk.

4. Fill liners 2/3 full. Bake 18–20 minutes. Cool and frost.

5. Beat buttercream ingredients until fluffy.

Soft Pretzels

Dough:

- 1 1/2 cups warm water
- 2 1/4 tsp active dry yeast
- 1 tsp salt
- 1 tbsp sugar
- 4 cups flour
- 2 tbsp butter (melted)

Baking Soda Bath:

- 1/2 cup baking soda
- 9 cups water

Topping:

- Coarse salt
- Optional: melted butter

Instructions:

1. Mix yeast and warm water. Let sit 5 minutes. Add salt, sugar, flour, and melted butter. Knead until smooth.
2. Let rise 1 hour. Preheat oven to 450°F (230°C).
3. Divide dough, roll into ropes, shape pretzels.

4. Boil each in soda bath for 30 seconds.

5. Bake 12–14 minutes. Brush with butter, sprinkle with salt.

Chocolate Lava Cakes

Ingredients:

- 1/2 cup butter
- 4 oz bittersweet chocolate
- 1 cup powdered sugar
- 2 eggs
- 2 egg yolks
- 6 tbsp flour
- Optional: vanilla or espresso powder

Instructions:

1. Preheat oven to 425°F (220°C). Grease and flour 4 ramekins.
2. Melt chocolate and butter together. Stir in sugar.
3. Whisk in eggs and yolks, then flour.
4. Divide into ramekins and bake 12–14 minutes.
5. Let sit 1 minute, then invert and serve warm.

Raspberry Almond Bars

Ingredients (Crust & Topping):

- 1 cup butter (cold, cubed)
- 2 cups flour
- 1/2 cup sugar
- 1/2 tsp salt

Filling:

- 3/4 cup raspberry jam
- 1/2 tsp almond extract
- 1/2 cup sliced almonds

Instructions:

1. Preheat oven to 350°F (175°C). Grease 8x8 pan.
2. Mix crust ingredients until crumbly. Press 2/3 into pan.
3. Spread jam mixed with almond extract. Crumble remaining dough on top.
4. Sprinkle almonds. Bake 35–40 minutes until golden. Cool completely.

Orange Poppy Seed Loaf

Ingredients:

- 1 1/2 cups flour
- 1/2 tsp baking soda
- 1/2 tsp salt
- 1 tbsp poppy seeds
- 1/2 cup butter (softened)
- 1 cup sugar
- 2 eggs
- 1 tbsp orange zest
- 1/4 cup orange juice
- 1/2 cup sour cream

Instructions:

1. Preheat oven to 350°F (175°C). Grease a loaf pan.
2. Cream butter and sugar. Add eggs and zest.
3. Mix in juice and sour cream.
4. Add dry ingredients and poppy seeds.
5. Bake 50–55 minutes. Cool and glaze if desired.

Chocolate Chip Scones

Ingredients:

- 2 cups flour
- 1/3 cup sugar
- 1 tbsp baking powder
- 1/2 tsp salt
- 1/2 cup cold butter (cubed)
- 1 cup chocolate chips
- 1/2 cup heavy cream
- 1 egg
- 1 tsp vanilla

Instructions:

1. Preheat oven to 400°F (200°C).
2. Mix dry ingredients. Cut in butter until crumbly.
3. Stir in chips. Mix cream, egg, and vanilla; add to dough.
4. Form a disk, cut into 8 wedges.
5. Bake 15–18 minutes until golden. Optional: brush with cream and sprinkle with sugar.

Lemon Bars

Crust:

- 1 cup butter (softened)
- 1/2 cup sugar
- 2 cups flour

Filling:

- 4 eggs
- 1 1/2 cups sugar
- 1/4 cup flour
- 2/3 cup lemon juice
- Optional: lemon zest

Instructions:

1. Preheat oven to 350°F (175°C). Line a 9x13 pan.
2. Mix crust ingredients, press into pan. Bake 15–20 minutes.
3. Whisk filling and pour over hot crust.
4. Bake 20–25 minutes until set. Cool completely. Dust with powdered sugar.

Almond Biscotti

Ingredients:

- 1 3/4 cups flour
- 1 tsp baking powder
- 1/2 tsp salt
- 1/2 cup sugar
- 1/2 cup sliced almonds
- 2 large eggs
- 1 tsp vanilla extract
- 1 tsp almond extract

Instructions:

1. Preheat oven to 350°F (175°C). Line a baking sheet with parchment paper.
2. Mix flour, baking powder, salt, and sugar. Stir in almonds.
3. Beat eggs and extracts, then mix into dry ingredients.
4. Shape dough into a log and bake 25–30 minutes.
5. Cool, slice into 1/2-inch pieces, and bake again for 10–12 minutes until crisp.

Sticky Toffee Pudding

Cake:

- 1 1/2 cups chopped dates
- 1 tsp baking soda
- 1/2 cup boiling water
- 1/2 cup butter (softened)
- 1/2 cup sugar
- 2 eggs
- 1 tsp vanilla extract
- 1 1/2 cups flour
- 1/2 tsp baking powder
- 1/4 tsp salt

Sauce:

- 1/2 cup butter
- 1 cup brown sugar
- 1/2 cup heavy cream
- 1 tsp vanilla extract

Instructions:

1. Preheat oven to 350°F (175°C). Grease a baking dish.

2. Pour boiling water over dates and baking soda, then let sit.

3. Cream butter and sugar. Add eggs and vanilla.

4. Stir in dry ingredients and date mixture. Pour into dish and bake 30–35 minutes.

5. For sauce: Melt butter, sugar, cream, and vanilla in a pan. Pour over warm pudding.

Cherry Clafoutis

Ingredients:

- 2 cups cherries (pitted)
- 1 cup milk
- 3/4 cup sugar
- 3 eggs
- 1 tsp vanilla extract
- 1/2 tsp almond extract
- 1/2 cup flour
- 1/4 tsp salt
- Powdered sugar for dusting

Instructions:

1. Preheat oven to 350°F (175°C). Grease a baking dish.
2. Arrange cherries in the dish.
3. Whisk milk, sugar, eggs, vanilla, almond extract, flour, and salt.
4. Pour batter over cherries and bake 40–45 minutes until puffed and golden.
5. Dust with powdered sugar before serving.

Irish Soda Bread

Ingredients:

- 4 cups flour
- 1 tsp baking soda
- 1 tsp salt
- 1/4 cup sugar
- 1 cup buttermilk
- 1/4 cup butter (cold, cubed)

Instructions:

1. Preheat oven to 375°F (190°C). Grease a baking sheet.
2. Mix dry ingredients. Cut in butter until crumbly.
3. Stir in buttermilk until just combined.
4. Shape into a round loaf, score the top, and bake for 35–45 minutes until golden.

Carrot Cake with Cream Cheese Frosting

Cake:

- 2 cups flour
- 1 tsp baking powder
- 1/2 tsp baking soda
- 1/2 tsp salt
- 1 tsp cinnamon
- 1/2 tsp nutmeg
- 3 eggs
- 1 1/2 cups sugar
- 1 cup vegetable oil
- 2 cups grated carrots
- 1 cup chopped walnuts (optional)

Frosting:

- 8 oz cream cheese (softened)
- 1/2 cup butter (softened)
- 4 cups powdered sugar
- 1 tsp vanilla extract

Instructions:

1. Preheat oven to 350°F (175°C). Grease two 9-inch cake pans.

2. Mix dry ingredients. Beat eggs, sugar, and oil, then stir in carrots and nuts.

3. Combine with dry ingredients and divide into pans.

4. Bake 25–30 minutes.

5. For frosting, beat cream cheese and butter. Gradually add powdered sugar and vanilla. Frost cooled cakes.

Gingerbread Loaf

Ingredients:

- 2 cups flour
- 1 tsp baking soda
- 1 tsp ground ginger
- 1/2 tsp cinnamon
- 1/4 tsp cloves
- 1/2 tsp salt
- 1/2 cup butter (softened)
- 1/2 cup brown sugar
- 1 egg
- 1 cup molasses
- 1/2 cup buttermilk

Instructions:

1. Preheat oven to 350°F (175°C). Grease a loaf pan.
2. Mix dry ingredients. Cream butter and sugar. Add egg, molasses, and buttermilk.
3. Gradually stir in dry ingredients.
4. Pour into pan and bake 55–60 minutes. Cool before slicing.

Cranberry Orange Muffins

Ingredients:

- 1 1/2 cups flour
- 1/2 cup sugar
- 2 tsp baking powder
- 1/4 tsp salt
- 1/2 tsp baking soda
- 1 egg
- 1/2 cup orange juice
- 1/4 cup vegetable oil
- 1 tsp orange zest
- 1 cup fresh cranberries

Instructions:

1. Preheat oven to 375°F (190°C). Line muffin tin.
2. Mix dry ingredients. In another bowl, whisk egg, juice, oil, and zest.
3. Stir wet into dry ingredients and fold in cranberries.
4. Spoon into muffin tin and bake 18–20 minutes.

Apple Pie

Crust:

- 2 1/2 cups flour
- 1 tsp salt
- 1 tbsp sugar
- 1 cup cold butter (cubed)
- 6–8 tbsp ice water

Filling:

- 6 cups peeled and sliced apples (Granny Smith or Honeycrisp)
- 1/2 cup sugar
- 1/4 cup brown sugar
- 1 tsp cinnamon
- 1/2 tsp nutmeg
- 2 tbsp flour
- 1 tbsp lemon juice

Instructions:

1. Preheat oven to 425°F (220°C).
2. For crust: Mix dry ingredients, cut in butter until crumbly. Gradually add water.
3. Roll out half of the dough and line a pie dish.

4. For filling: Mix apples with sugars, spices, flour, and lemon juice.

5. Pour into crust, top with second dough layer, crimp edges, and cut slits.

6. Bake 45–50 minutes until golden.

Chocolate Zucchini Cake

Ingredients:

- 1 1/2 cups flour
- 1/2 cup cocoa powder
- 1 tsp baking powder
- 1/2 tsp baking soda
- 1/4 tsp salt
- 1 tsp cinnamon
- 1/2 cup butter (softened)
- 1/2 cup sugar
- 1/2 cup brown sugar
- 2 eggs
- 1 tsp vanilla extract
- 1 1/2 cups grated zucchini (excess moisture squeezed out)
- 1/2 cup sour cream
- 1/2 cup chocolate chips

Instructions:

1. Preheat oven to 350°F (175°C). Grease a 9x13 baking dish.
2. In a bowl, mix flour, cocoa powder, baking powder, baking soda, salt, and cinnamon.

3. Beat butter, sugar, and brown sugar until creamy. Add eggs and vanilla.

4. Gradually mix in the dry ingredients. Add zucchini and sour cream, then fold in chocolate chips.

5. Pour batter into prepared dish and bake for 30–35 minutes. Cool completely.

Butterscotch Blondies

Ingredients:

- 1 1/2 cups brown sugar
- 1/2 cup butter (softened)
- 2 eggs
- 1 tsp vanilla extract
- 2 cups flour
- 1 tsp baking powder
- 1/2 tsp salt
- 1 cup butterscotch chips

Instructions:

1. Preheat oven to 350°F (175°C). Grease a 9x9 baking dish.
2. Cream butter and sugar together. Add eggs and vanilla.
3. Mix in flour, baking powder, and salt. Fold in butterscotch chips.
4. Pour batter into dish and bake for 20–25 minutes. Cool before cutting into squares.

Pineapple Upside-Down Cake

Ingredients:

- 1/4 cup butter (melted)
- 1/2 cup brown sugar
- 8–10 pineapple rings (drained)
- Maraschino cherries

Cake:

- 1 1/2 cups flour
- 1 tsp baking powder
- 1/2 tsp baking soda
- 1/4 tsp salt
- 1/2 cup butter (softened)
- 1 cup sugar
- 2 eggs
- 1 tsp vanilla extract
- 1/2 cup sour cream

Instructions:

1. Preheat oven to 350°F (175°C). Grease a 9-inch round cake pan.

2. Pour melted butter into the pan and sprinkle with brown sugar. Arrange pineapple rings and cherries.

3. For the cake, mix dry ingredients. Cream butter and sugar, then add eggs and vanilla.

4. Add dry ingredients and sour cream, then pour over pineapple.

5. Bake for 35–40 minutes. Cool for 10 minutes, then flip onto a plate.

Coconut Macaroons

Ingredients:

- 2 1/2 cups shredded coconut
- 2/3 cup sugar
- 2 large egg whites
- 1 tsp vanilla extract
- 1/4 tsp salt

Instructions:

1. Preheat oven to 325°F (165°C). Line a baking sheet with parchment paper.
2. Mix coconut, sugar, egg whites, vanilla, and salt until combined.
3. Form the mixture into small mounds and place on the sheet.
4. Bake for 15–20 minutes until golden brown. Cool completely.

Pumpkin Muffins

Ingredients:

- 1 1/2 cups flour
- 1 tsp baking powder
- 1/2 tsp baking soda
- 1/2 tsp salt
- 1 tsp cinnamon
- 1/2 tsp nutmeg
- 1/4 tsp ground ginger
- 1/2 cup sugar
- 1/2 cup brown sugar
- 2 eggs
- 1 cup pumpkin puree
- 1/2 cup vegetable oil
- 1 tsp vanilla extract

Instructions:

1. Preheat oven to 350°F (175°C). Line a muffin tin.
2. Mix dry ingredients. In another bowl, whisk eggs, sugar, brown sugar, pumpkin, oil, and vanilla.
3. Combine wet and dry ingredients, and stir until just combined.

4. Fill muffin cups and bake for 20–25 minutes. Cool before serving.

Marble Pound Cake

Ingredients:

- 2 cups flour
- 1 tsp baking powder
- 1/4 tsp salt
- 1 cup butter (softened)
- 1 1/2 cups sugar
- 4 large eggs
- 1 tsp vanilla extract
- 1/4 cup milk
- 1/4 cup cocoa powder
- 2 tbsp hot water

Instructions:

1. Preheat oven to 350°F (175°C). Grease and flour a loaf pan.
2. Mix flour, baking powder, and salt. Cream butter and sugar, then add eggs one at a time.
3. Alternate adding flour mixture and milk, beginning and ending with flour.
4. In a separate bowl, dissolve cocoa in hot water. Take half the batter and mix with cocoa.
5. Alternate spooning vanilla and chocolate batters into the pan. Swirl with a knife.

6. Bake for 50-60 minutes. Cool completely.

Rustic Berry Galette

Crust:

- 1 1/4 cups flour
- 1/4 tsp salt
- 1/2 cup butter (cold, cubed)
- 3–4 tbsp ice water

Filling:

- 2 cups mixed berries (strawberries, raspberries, blueberries)
- 1/4 cup sugar
- 1 tbsp cornstarch
- 1 tbsp lemon juice
- 1/2 tsp vanilla extract

Instructions:

1. Preheat oven to 375°F (190°C). Roll out dough on parchment paper into a rough circle.
2. Toss berries with sugar, cornstarch, lemon juice, and vanilla.
3. Place berries in the center of the dough, leaving a border. Fold edges over fruit.
4. Bake for 35–40 minutes. Cool before serving.

Maple Pecan Scones

Ingredients:

- 2 cups flour
- 1/2 cup sugar
- 1 tbsp baking powder
- 1/2 tsp salt
- 1/2 cup butter (cold, cubed)
- 1/2 cup chopped pecans
- 1/2 cup heavy cream
- 1/4 cup maple syrup
- 1 tsp vanilla extract

Instructions:

1. Preheat oven to 400°F (200°C). Line a baking sheet with parchment paper.
2. Mix dry ingredients. Cut in butter until crumbly. Stir in pecans.
3. Mix cream, maple syrup, and vanilla, then stir into the dry mixture.
4. Form dough into a disk, cut into wedges, and bake for 15–18 minutes. Cool slightly.

Chocolate Babka

Ingredients:

Dough:

- 3 cups flour
- 1/4 cup sugar
- 1 packet active dry yeast
- 1 tsp salt
- 1/2 cup warm milk
- 2 eggs
- 1/2 cup butter (softened)

Filling:

- 1 cup chocolate chips
- 1/4 cup cocoa powder
- 1/4 cup sugar
- 1/4 cup butter (melted)

Syrup:

- 1/4 cup water
- 1/4 cup sugar

Instructions:

1. Preheat oven to 350°F (175°C). Grease a loaf pan.

2. Mix warm milk, yeast, and a pinch of sugar. Let it sit for 5 minutes to activate.

3. In a large bowl, combine flour, sugar, salt, eggs, and yeast mixture. Add butter and knead into a dough. Let rise for 1–2 hours.

4. Roll out dough into a rectangle. Mix the filling ingredients and spread over the dough.

5. Roll dough into a log, cut it in half lengthwise, and twist the two halves together.

6. Place in the pan and let rise for 30 minutes. Bake for 30–40 minutes.

7. For the syrup: Boil water and sugar, then drizzle over the warm babka.

Chai-Spiced Oat Bars

Ingredients:

- 2 cups rolled oats
- 1 cup flour
- 1/2 tsp baking soda
- 1/2 tsp salt
- 1/2 tsp cinnamon
- 1/4 tsp cardamom
- 1/4 tsp ginger
- 1/4 tsp cloves
- 1/2 cup butter (softened)
- 1/2 cup brown sugar
- 1 egg
- 1/2 cup honey
- 1/4 cup milk
- 1 tsp vanilla extract

Instructions:

1. Preheat oven to 350°F (175°C). Grease a 9x9 baking dish.
2. In a bowl, combine oats, flour, baking soda, salt, and spices.

3. Beat butter, brown sugar, egg, honey, milk, and vanilla until smooth.

4. Stir in dry ingredients, then spread into the dish.

5. Bake for 20–25 minutes, until golden and firm. Cool completely before cutting into bars.

Bread Pudding

Ingredients:

- 4 cups cubed stale bread
- 2 cups milk
- 3 eggs
- 1/2 cup sugar
- 1 tsp vanilla extract
- 1/2 tsp cinnamon
- 1/4 tsp salt
- 1/2 cup raisins (optional)
- 2 tbsp butter (cubed)

Instructions:

1. Preheat oven to 350°F (175°C). Grease a baking dish.
2. In a bowl, whisk together milk, eggs, sugar, vanilla, cinnamon, and salt.
3. Add bread cubes and let soak for 15 minutes. Stir in raisins.
4. Pour mixture into the baking dish and dot with butter.
5. Bake for 35–40 minutes, until set and golden. Serve warm with whipped cream or a drizzle of caramel sauce.

Lavender Shortbread Cookies

Ingredients:

- 2 cups flour
- 1/2 cup powdered sugar
- 1 tsp lavender buds (dried)
- 1/4 tsp salt
- 1 cup butter (softened)
- 1 tsp vanilla extract

Instructions:

1. Preheat oven to 325°F (165°C). Line a baking sheet with parchment paper.
2. In a bowl, combine flour, sugar, lavender, and salt.
3. Beat in butter and vanilla until the dough forms.
4. Roll out dough and cut into desired shapes.
5. Place on the baking sheet and bake for 12–15 minutes, until lightly golden. Let cool.

Cherry Pie Bars

Ingredients:

Crust:

- 1 1/2 cups flour
- 1/2 cup sugar
- 1/2 tsp baking powder
- 1/4 tsp salt
- 1/2 cup butter (cold, cubed)
- 1 egg (beaten)

Filling:

- 2 cups fresh or canned cherry filling (or homemade)
- 1 tbsp cornstarch (optional, for thickening)

Instructions:

1. Preheat oven to 350°F (175°C). Grease a 9x9 baking dish.
2. In a bowl, combine flour, sugar, baking powder, and salt. Cut in cold butter until the mixture is crumbly. Stir in the egg.
3. Press 2/3 of the dough mixture into the bottom of the dish to form the crust.
4. Spread the cherry filling evenly over the dough.
5. Crumble the remaining dough over the top and bake for 35–40 minutes until golden brown. Cool before cutting into bars.

Almond Cake with Citrus Glaze

Ingredients:

Cake:

- 1 1/2 cups almond flour
- 1 cup all-purpose flour
- 1 tsp baking powder
- 1/4 tsp salt
- 1/2 cup butter (softened)
- 1 cup sugar
- 3 large eggs
- 1 tsp vanilla extract
- 1/2 cup milk

Citrus Glaze:

- 1/2 cup powdered sugar
- 2 tbsp orange juice (or lemon juice)
- Zest of 1 orange or lemon

Instructions:

1. Preheat oven to 350°F (175°C). Grease an 8-inch round cake pan.
2. Mix almond flour, all-purpose flour, baking powder, and salt in a bowl.

3. Cream butter and sugar, then add eggs one at a time, followed by vanilla.

4. Gradually add dry ingredients, alternating with milk, and stir until combined.

5. Pour batter into the pan and bake for 30–35 minutes, until a toothpick comes out clean.

6. While the cake cools, whisk together powdered sugar, citrus juice, and zest.

7. Drizzle the glaze over the cooled cake before serving.

Classic Sugar Cookies

Ingredients:

- 2 3/4 cups flour
- 1 tsp baking soda
- 1/2 tsp baking powder
- 1 cup butter (softened)
- 1 1/2 cups sugar
- 1 egg
- 1 tsp vanilla extract
- 1/2 tsp almond extract (optional)
- 1/4 cup sugar (for rolling)

Instructions:

1. Preheat oven to 350°F (175°C). Line a baking sheet with parchment paper.
2. Mix flour, baking soda, and baking powder.
3. Cream butter and sugar, then beat in the egg and extracts.
4. Gradually add dry ingredients until dough forms.
5. Roll dough into balls, then roll in sugar. Place on the baking sheet and press lightly.
6. Bake for 8–10 minutes until edges are golden. Cool on a wire rack.

Sweet Potato Biscuits

Ingredients:

- 2 cups flour
- 1 tbsp baking powder
- 1/2 tsp salt
- 1/2 tsp cinnamon (optional)
- 1/4 tsp nutmeg (optional)
- 1/2 cup butter (cold, cubed)
- 1 cup mashed sweet potatoes (cooked and cooled)
- 1/4 cup milk

Instructions:

1. Preheat oven to 425°F (220°C). Line a baking sheet with parchment paper.
2. Mix flour, baking powder, salt, cinnamon, and nutmeg in a bowl.
3. Cut in butter until the mixture is crumbly.
4. Stir in mashed sweet potatoes and milk until just combined.
5. Drop spoonfuls of dough onto the baking sheet and bake for 12–15 minutes, until golden. Cool slightly before serving.

Lemon Ricotta Cookies

Ingredients:

Cookies:

- 2 1/2 cups flour
- 1 1/2 tsp baking powder
- 1/4 tsp salt
- 1 cup ricotta cheese
- 1/2 cup butter (softened)
- 1 cup sugar
- 2 eggs
- Zest of 1 lemon
- 2 tbsp lemon juice
- 1 tsp vanilla extract

Glaze:

- 1 cup powdered sugar
- 2 tbsp lemon juice

Instructions:

1. Preheat oven to 350°F (175°C). Line a baking sheet with parchment paper.
2. Mix flour, baking powder, and salt.

3. Beat ricotta, butter, and sugar until creamy. Add eggs, lemon zest, lemon juice, and vanilla.

4. Gradually add dry ingredients until just combined.

5. Drop spoonfuls of dough onto the baking sheet and bake for 10–12 minutes, until light golden.

6. For the glaze: whisk powdered sugar and lemon juice until smooth. Drizzle over cooled cookies.

www.ingramcontent.com/pod-product-compliance
Lightning Source LLC
LaVergne TN
LVHW081619060526
838201LV00054B/2321